UNSTUCK

UNSTUCK

CYNTHIA JETER-CLEMENTS

GET WRITE PUBLISHING

Unstuck

Copyright © 2019 by Cynthia Jeter-Clements.

Unless otherwise indicated, scripture references are from the New International Version and the King James Bible Version.

ISBN: 978-1-7337020-9-6

Cover Design: USEntarprise

Get Write Publishing
2770 Main Street – Suite 147
Frisco, TX 75033

TABLE OF CONTENTS

FOREWORD

Cynthia Jeter Clements is a lover of people and a humble servant of God. A faithful supporter and powerhouse preacher in her own right, her passion for ministry is undeniable. I believe that her book, *Unstuck* will expand her reach into new territories across the globe.

Cynthia is mantled for the masses. Through her own testimony of trials and triumphs, she provides biblical and practical principles to help set the captives free. In *Unstuck*, Cynthia uproots some of the hidden culprits that have stalled multiple generations and plants seeds of progress. *Unstuck* will pull readers out of complacency and launch them into destiny.

Dr. Medina Pullings
Pastor
United Nations Church
Jesus Girl International

Praise for "Unstuck"

Over the years, I have watched Cynthia Jeter help countless people move forward. She has a gift to see dormant value and purpose in people and help bring it to life. At some point, we've all gotten stuck in the pain and disappointment of yesterday or our current situation, but far too many stay stuck!

In *UnStuck*, Cynthia first shares her own personal and painful experiences and then shows how to move past them. We cannot control everything that happens to us, or change past bad decisions, but we can move forward into a better future. *UnStuck* is a practical and powerful roadmap to help move past yesterday's pain and into a life of greater joy, purpose, and power.

Pastor Jack Redmond
Church Mobilization Pastor
Christ Church
Co-Author of *In My Father's Shoes –
Healing the Father Wound*

It has been my pleasure to connect with Cynthia in the journey of ministry. During our ordained appointment, kindred spirits were blossomed.

I have witnessed her gifting, heart, and commitment to release women from the prisons of generational curses. I am excited that *Unstuck* is yet another avenue for her to share with the body of Christ for the purpose of experiencing the freedom to move toward their God-given destiny.

Jodie McCoy
Co-Pastor
Hope International Church

I am blessed to have a daughter-in-law that loves Jesus and wants to see the advancement of His Kingdom here on earth. I admire her heart to serve and to see the lives of people transformed by the Word of God. Her transparency in her personal journey will help build people from the inside out.

Through my years in ministry, I have come to understand the power of serving and loving people. Cynthia has both qualities. She sets the needs of her family as a priority and places the ministry second. *Unstuck* will move people out of park and shift them into drive to be all that God called them to be.

Bishop William Lee III
Church of the Living God
New Full Gospel, Germany

It has been a blessing of encouragement, belief, and joy that God placed His beautiful servant and woman of God, Cynthia Jeter-Clements, in my life. Cynthia has repositioned herself as an incredible leader and continues to take others with her as she soars high as a Kingdom woman. As one of her leaders, I have appreciated her ability to listen. Many people are able to hear, but few are capable to really listen. Cynthia is a great leader who is unafraid to take ownership and accepts the responsibility of encouraging others to live the life of their dreams.

Cynthia teaches women how to fail forward without giving up and how they must rise above opposition. She is proof that tough times don't last, but tough people *do*. Cynthia is a living example of maximizing her potential and becoming "unstuck." I am so very proud of Cynthia and I am confident that God is using her for His purpose.

Beatrice G. Powell
Motivational & Inspirational Speaker
National Sales Director Emeritus
Mary Kay, Inc.

Acknowledgements

To my husband, who has always supported me in business and ministry. You have been the best husband a woman could ever dream of. I waited 37 years to find a love like yours and it was worth the wait. I am happy to share this life with you and excited that we get to share our story together.

To my daughters, Emani & Hannah. I have always tried my best to be a better human to break boundaries and limitations off my thinking to leave a legacy for both of you. Life will throw a lot of curve balls, but we must find the strength to learn the lesson to help and be a blessing in the lives of others. I love you both dearly. Please share this book and others with my unborn grandchildren and great grandchildren.

To all of my mentors and encouragers over the years. Pastor Jack Redmond, thank you for believing in me when I did not believe in myself and seeing beyond where I was as a baby in Christ Jesus 15 years ago.

To the late Karen D. Thomas, thank you for praying for me and listening to my hopes and dreams.

To my father Andre Jeter Jr., thank you for always reminding me that I can do anything I put my mind to and for me to strive to be all that God has called me to be.

To my late grandmother, Inez Jeter for raising me after my parents split, and for always loving on me and teaching me how to pray.

INTRODUCTION

It is God's will that we excel in every area of our lives. The Bible says: **Beloved, I wish above all things that thou mayest prosper and be in health, even as thy soul prospereth** (3 John 2-5). This is one of my favorite scriptures because it talks about us prospering in every area of our lives—including our health—even as our souls prosper. It is clear that God wants us to prosper in our vocation, health, finances, relationships, and the soul.

Many people want to prosper but cannot because they are STUCK. This can happen to anyone. The purpose of this book is to help you become **UNSTUCK**. I will use personal testimonies about how I was stuck in certain areas of my life and walked through the process of releasing myself to a place of freedom and redemption. The Bible reads: **Now the Lord is the Spirit, and where the Spirit of the Lord is, there is freedom** (2 Corinthians 3:17). As situations occur in life, we must

1

all find ways to escape the deep dark places that can result from life's tragedies.

I am fully aware that many things can happen to people that they are not personally responsible for. Some may have been victimized at a young age. Children are often mishandled and mistreated. I can speak from experience but I can also tell you that God is ready and willing to help anyone to heal and pick up the broken pieces. It is my desire that you will allow my personal testimony to help you find freedom and hope in your situation. Your past pain can no longer hold your future in bondage. You are free to be unstuck.

Chapter 1

THIS LIFE

Every human being on planted earth was born without being asked to come to here. Think about it. We don't get to pick our parents, we don't get to pick our gender, we don't get to pick our race or financial affiliations. We have no choice in the matter. The Bible states: **Before I formed you in the womb I knew you, before you were born I set you apart; I appointed you as a prophet to the nations** (Jeremiah 1:5). God was talking to the prophet Jeremiah; however, the same scriptures are true for us.

As a child, I questioned God. I wanted to know how and why He gave me the parents that I have. My mother, Norbratina Marie Arrindell, was diagnosed with schizophrenia at the age of 25. My father, Andre J. Jeter, suffered from drug addiction until 7 years ago. I can remember my father being on drugs for most of my childhood and my mother having severe episodes that drove her to mental institutions.

I had some serious questions for the Man upstairs. I always believed in God, even at a young age. It was the only hope I had growing up in such a hostile environment. Talking to God was my escape.

When I got older, and started to study the Word of God. After reading Jeremiah 1:5, I realized that God had a reason for choosing my parents. I just had to find out why.

What gave me hope was knowing that God thought about me while I was being created in my mother's womb. He created me and He loved me. Later in life, God would begin to use my mistakes, misfortunes, and successes to help me see just how much He loved me and to help other people to receive God's love.

God loves everyone born, even those who don't make it out the womb. As a mother of two children, I know firsthand what it feels like to have a life growing inside of your body. I believe God loves us from the day of conception, despite the details.

It is our job to find out why we are here, and use the circumstances we face to live the kind of lives that please God. When we bring honor to God, we find happiness, hope, peace, love and comfort. I am not saying life in Christ is easy or that we will not have problems. When we search for God's love, He comforts us through all trials and tribulations.

My parents married at a very young age, mainly because my mother was pregnant with my older brother. In those days, people did not have children out of wedlock (if the parents could help it). I was the middle child and the only girl of three children.

I can remember looking at wedding pictures of my parents. I saw how confused they looked at the altar. I can clearly understand why now that I am an adult. I could not imagine getting married at 16, which was my mother's age when she got married. My father was 19. It is absolutely crazy to me to imagine that a 16-year-old and a 19-year-old are ready for marriage; however, people made situations like that work back then. Both of my grandparents did. In the 1950s, things started to change just like they are changing now.

In order for me to try to understand my life, I had to first examine the lives of my parents and my grandparents. This gave me a clearer understanding of who I was, how I got here, my generational blessings, and family curses (of which we will talk about later). When I thought about their lives, deep sorrow came into my heart. I developed an appreciation for my parents, despite their failures.

When I considered my mother's childhood, I realized why she could not express feelings of love towards me. I understood why she was abusive, both verbally and physically. Her own history of childhood abuse did not give her the right to harm me, but it did give me a clear understanding of the abusive cycle that took root in my family.

As I got older and my relationship with the Lord grew stronger, my questions changed from "Why, God?" to "How can I change this, and make it stop?" It is important to learn that as we mature, so should our understanding. Unfortunately, many people are not able to grow because they become stuck at the places in life where hurt and trauma occurred. They may have grown physically, but they have not moved past the hurt and pain they experienced at different points in their lives.

It is not God's plan for us to be or feel stuck. As we read in the Bible in John 10:10, **The thief does not come except to steal, and to kill, and to destroy. I have come that they may have life, and that they may have it more abundantly.** It is clear that there is an evil force and a host of demons that come to steal our future and to take what rightfully belongs to us. God gave us tools to take back what the devil stole, to restore our hearts and minds, and to give us a promised future.

Although we cannot go back and undo the things that were done to us or the things that we have done to others, God can release the hurt and pain from our hearts and help us to move forward. He wants to move us to the place of freedom and redemption. 2 Corinthians 3:17 tells us: **Now the Lord is the Spirit, and where the Spirit of the Lord is, there is freedom**. This gives us the freedom to love and forgive. This freedom also gives us the mind and heart to make the right choices.

My parents came from normal, middle class backgrounds. My grandparents on both sides were married until death. The marriage of my grandparents was not perfect or without problems.

The only grandparent that had a relationship with the Lord was my father's mother, Inez Jeter. Inez had a huge impact on our family. She made Jesus a part of all of our lives and reminded us about the importance of us giving our lives to Him. She kept us in church and made her faith real in our lives, and in the lives of others around her. She was the glue that kept my family together, even when my parents separated and my brothers and I went to live with her. She raised me from the age of 9 until 17, when she passed away.

My grandmother was my first introduction to prayer and knowing the power of the name Jesus. Through the many miracles I seen happen in her life, I had no doubt in my mind about the power of prayer and that my Savior lives. However, I did not give my life to Christ until I was 26 years old. It was not until then that I realized how much my childhood negatively affected my life.

It took me years to cope with having a mother that suffered from mental illness and a father on drugs. I was not able to have a relationship with my mother due to her mental health conditions. My grandmother raised us the best way she could. I never missed a meal. She kept me dressed in the latest fashions. She even took me to the hair salon twice a month! I also traveled with her occasionally. She tried her best to give me the things I could not get from my parents and show me the love I was missing.

Inez did an excellent job raising us. I thank God often for having her in my life and the impact she had. The truth is, if she had not raised me for those years, I probably would not have the relationship I have today with the Lord. This is a reminder of one of my favorite scriptures, **"And we know that all things work together for good to them that love God, to them who are the called according to his purpose"** (Romans 8:28).

Growing up with parents who had major personal struggles was not easy for me; however, I thank God that during those years I could sense Him around me and protecting me. I have a place in my heart for people who struggle with mental illnesses because my mother suffered for years with mental health issues. I have a place in my heart for people addicted to drugs, because my father struggled with drug addiction for years.

God can use your pain to develop your heart to help people if you choose not to become stuck on the pain and focus on the purpose instead. Unfortunately, many people never get past the hurt.

I know what it feels like to be abused by a parent. I was abused by my mother for years before I told anyone. I know what it's like to wait for your father to come and pick you up but he never shows up. I know the damage a child experiences growing up with both parents having serious issues and feeling worthless because God chose them as your parents. I felt like I would never amount to anything because of the examples of my parents set.

Most people feel like they should be able to look to their parents for guidance and support. But what happens when your parents are not available to give you the tools you need to be successful in life? Who do you turn to? **A father to the fatherless, a defender of widows, is God in his holy dwelling. God sets the lonely in families, he leads out the prisoners with singing; but the rebellious live in a sun-scorched land** (Psalm 68:5-6). God, the Creator of heaven and earth, is concerned about your life and your future.

I remember as a little girl wondering why I was going through those things. Why did those mean things happen to me? I never got an answer, but I can tell you as I look back; God was with me. I would not wish hurt and pain on anyone; however, my experience is the reason that I can help so many people today.

I refuse to be stuck in my past. If I allow my history or the people who hurt me to control my heart and mind, then the enemy gets the victory. The Bible reads: **For our struggle is not against flesh and blood, but against the rulers, against the authorities, against the powers of this dark world and against the spiritual forces of evil in the heavenly realms** (Ephesians 6:12). Truthfully, people hurt people, but the force behind the hurt is the evil one. I try to keep this at the forefront of my mind when someone does something to hurt me.

I realize there is a stronger force working behind a person's evil ways. This force is stronger than the person causing the hurt and pain. Many times, people who cause severe hurt and pain in the lives of others don't even know why they did it after the damage has been done. I am not encouraging you to act like it never happened, but allow your heart and mind to find out what caused the action.

At the age of 16, I tried to figure out why my mother abused me. I remember asking God about it. After my parents lost custody of us, my grandmother became our caregiver.

We would often have visits from social workers. My social worker, Mrs. Green, came to visit me one day and she asked my grandmother if she could take me to lunch. Mrs. Green was a well-educated, classy Christian woman. I respected and admired her. In fact, she would often pick me up and take me places with her outside of working hours. That was a strategic move of God.

On one particular lunch outing, Mrs. Green took me to the public library. She gave me a few books to read about schizophrenia, which was the mental health condition my mother suffered from. She also printed out articles for me to read. She helped me understand my mother's illness from a medical standpoint.

I remember sitting in the library, crying and thinking to myself, *how can a person live like this?* The hurt and pain I had towards my mother immediately left. Mrs. Green hugged me and began to cry with me. She also prayed with me.

I started to feel sorry for my mother. At that point, I made a decision in my life to be unstuck in my heart. I remember wanting to care for and protect my mother, and I did from that point on.

Mrs. Green helped me understand what my mother was going through in her mind. However, it was my grandmother who explained it to me spiritually and helped me understand generational curses. As I got older, the pieces of the puzzle started to connect. As I matured in my faith in God, He began to help me understand my life and the life of my parents better. This helped me to eventually surrender to the Holy Spirit to create the life God destined for me.

Through prayer, reading the Word of God, and the community of believers in Christ Jesus, I learned that others went through great trials in their lives and were able to be victorious. I was determined to come out on the winning side of hurt and childhood trauma. The Bible reads: **And they have defeated him by the blood of the Lamb and by their testimony. And they did not love their lives so much that they were afraid to die** (Revelations 12:11).

I had to make a choice daily. I had to die to what happened to me. I realize that it was a part of my life, but it did not have to be who I am. I had to die to negative feelings and emotions. I was not going to stay stuck. I was going to allow the Holy Spirit to heal my heart and walk me through the necessary process of becoming "unstuck." God will send people into our lives at different points to help us pull the pieces together. The question is, do we really want the help or do we want to stay stuck?

Chapter 2

LIFE CHOICES

Things always seem much clearer in hindsight. The Bible says: **Let no one deceive himself. If anyone among you thinks that he is wise in this age, let him become a fool that he may become wise** (1 Corinthians 3:18). I think this is the perfect scripture for certain choices we make. A lot of the wrong decisions that we make in life are a result of having the wrong mindset.

When we grow up with a dysfunctional childhood, we tend to blame every single choice that we make on our upbringing. I do agree that a lot of our choices are a direct result of how we were raised and groomed as children. The environment we grew up in can help set a clear path for us to live the kind of life that Jesus Christ died for us to have. The Bible says: **The thief cometh not but to steal and to kill and to destroy. I am come that they**

might have life, and that they might have it more abundantly (John 10:10).

Jesus Christ clearly stated that He came to give us an abundant life. This means that every hurtful thing we experienced as a child did not come from Him, it was a result of "the thief." It is important to understand that humanity has a thief, adversary, manipulator, and a liar against what is true and Holy. This spirit is alive today.

The Bible reads: **For we do not wrestle against flesh and blood, but against principalities, against powers, against the rulers of the darkness of this age, against spiritual hosts of wickedness in the heavenly places** (Ephesians 6:12). This scripture is clear on who our fight is with—and believe me, this fight starts as early as childhood and even before we are born. In a loving environment, our upbringing can help foster the perfect will and plan Jesus has for our lives; however, when we are raised with dysfunction, we must clearly understand the source behind the hurt, pain, and trauma.

I am not saying that people who hurt others should not be held accountable for their actions. We have to understand that the hurt and pain inflicted on our lives goes deeper than even the person committing the pain can understand. The saying is true ... hurt people do hurt other people. We have to take time to get to the root of a problem understand how or why certain things happened in our lives. This can provide some comfort, but even if we don't get answers to understand how, or why we can trust in the above scripture in Ephesians 6:12.

The trust we have in God and His Word will actually heal a broken heart. I cannot tell you how deeply hurt I was as a child when my father would make promises that he could not keep; however, when I discovered the Word of God and read: **For all the promises of God are "Yes" in Christ. And so through Him, our "Amen" is spoken to the glory of God** (2 Corinthians 1:20). These promises did something to my heart and mind. They helped me understand that even though my biological father was unable to give me the love and attention I needed as a child; I had a Heavenly Father who adored me. I did not have to remain stuck in the disappointments of being let down again and again by my earthly father. I often ask myself and God, "Is there is something from my biological father that you needed to create me?" I laugh at this sometimes, but I really want to know.

Growing up with a father in and out my life, insecurities developed within me. I did not feel protected when he was absent. Because of his drug abuse, when he *was* around, I did not know which personality I would get. This dysfunctional relationship led to a lot of wrong dating decisions. I did not make wise choices when it came to men. I dated the wrong men based on perception and the relationship I had with my father.

My father was very smart but made a lot of wrong choices. I do remember my father going to work at times. He was a functioning drug user for many years until he lost his job.

After my parents separated (they never divorced), I went to live with my father's mother. It seemed as if my grandmother Inez was raising me and my father at the same time. As a child, seeing my grandmother consistently correct my father caused me to develop a lack of respect for him and the male gender as a whole. My grandmother was such a spiritually strong and determined woman that it became difficult for me to see how a man could benefit my life on an ongoing basis. Our dysfunctional father/daughter relationship resulted in me being "stuck" for a very long time.

It was not until the birth of my second child at the age of 30 that I really started to pay attention to the role my father played in my life. It directly affected the choices I made with men.

When I was 16, I received healing from my mother wounds. I remember that day like it was yesterday. The anger that I had towards her turned into deep love and concern for her wellbeing. I decided to love her despite any physical and mental abuse she inflicted upon me as a child. After I put myself in her shoes, all of the hurt and pain went away. I could feel my heart change towards my mother that day. The Bible says: **I will give you a new heart and put a new spirit in you; I will remove from you your heart of stone and give you a heart of flesh** (Ezekiel 36:26). I could physically feel my chest caving in as hurt and pain left my heart.

There are times when God in His infinite power will compel you to become unstuck. You will not need a therapist or a psychologist. You will not need countless hours in counseling sessions. Those things are needed at certain points in our lives, but there are times when the power of God will come and perform heart surgery on you. The Bible reads: **He heals the brokenhearted and binds up their wounds** (Psalm 147:3). I can tell you firsthand that I have experienced the power of a heart healed by God. He is alive; actively working and willing to heal your heart.

Sometimes being in a "stuck" place is comfortable. It was convenient for me to make my own choices when it came to dating because my flesh wanted it. After having my first child at 19, recovering from the hurt and pain of that relationship made it easy for me to move on at 20 years old.

I learned a few things about making right choices the hard way. I can clearly remember working in corporate America and not making enough money to take care of myself or my daughter. Instead of praying and waiting on God to give me a promotion, I took matters into my own hands. I worked as a receptionist by day. At night, I would sell clothing taken from high-end clothing stores. I was making double the money that my corporate job was paying.

I found out how to make fast money and was stuck in the wrong place. It all came crashing down when I was 24. I got arrested and had to spend time and money in and out of courthouses. I was pleading with the judge not to send me to prison for 2 or 3 years. I was ultimately sentenced to 45 days in prison, of which I served 30 days in jail. It was the worst and best 30 days of my life!

I was not raised to steal or do illegal things. After I did some soul-searching, I had to identify how that behavior started. Why did I want to take the easy way out and where did that decision come from? After spending time in prayer, the Holy Spirit showed me clearly where it came from.

When I was around 6 or 7, my father stole something from the grocery store while we were out with my mother. It was a joke to my father; however, it planted a seed in my mind. When the opportunity came for me to make fast money, getting something for nothing was planted in my subconscious mind. That is exactly what came out.

I thank God for His wisdom that helped me understand why I was able to fall into the trap. I was able to make better choices for myself and my daughter from that point forward. Even so, my father issue was not addressed completely.

At the age of 26, I promised God that if He would bless me with a good paying job, I would give my life to Him. That was a crazy request! Who am I to ask God for a trade-off for my salvation? God already gave His Son, Jesus Christ to die for my sins. Who am I to bargain with God? The Bible says: **For God so loved the world that he gave his one and only Son, that whoever believes in him shall not perish but have eternal life** (John 3:16).

I am amazed that God heard a sinner's prayer that day. Six months after that request, I started a good paying job. I was able to purchase my first home four years later! It took courage for me to pray such a bold prayer. I guess God knew my heart.

I cannot tell you why God answered such a self-centered prayer, other than the love He had for me and others. There are times that God will even answer childish prayers to let us know that He is listening to us, as long as our hearts are in the right place. At the time, I really needed a job to take care of myself and my daughter. I had no idea that He would bless me with a job making good money at a top accounting firm.

It took courage for me to believe God for a good job after everything I had gone through in the criminal justice system. I believe that there are people reading this book right now who are believing God for more but, based to your past, you are afraid to ask. I believe that after you read this book, you will be **unstuck**.

I had to dig deep and trust God to bring increase into my life to take care of myself and my daughter. I had no other alternative. I want you to ask God for exactly what you want from a sincere place. God will give us what we ask for when we ask Him with the right heart. The Bible reads: **If you abide in me, and my words abide in you, ask whatever you wish, and it will be done for you** (John 15:7).

It is easy to look at what we do not have and measure that against the goodness of God. It is easy to measure God's blessings by the level of goodness in our lives. We could never measure up to who God is and His blessings; however, we can ask believing that if we are in need, God will provide.

Do not compare how you are now or what you have done in the past to who God is. The Bible says: **Before I formed you in the womb I knew you, before you were born I set you apart; I appointed you as a prophet to the nations** (Jeremiah 1:5). God was speaking to the prophet Jeremiah. The prophet was afraid to go where God said because of his age. However, God told Jeremiah about who He was and that He knew everything about him even before He placed him in his mother's womb.

It is amazing to know that God knew every mistake, choice, or bad behavior that we would make, yet He still loves us as His own. God also knew every wrong thing done to us at the hands of others, yet He still qualifies us as His own masterpiece. God is not surprised by what we have done, so He sent His son to give us a bright future and hope. The Bible tells us: **"For I know the plans I have for you," declares the Lord, "plans to prosper you and not to harm you, plans to give you hope and a future"** (Jeremiah 29:11).

It does not matter what other people say about you. It does not matter what other people had planned for your life. God said He has plans to prosper you and not harm you and to give you hope and a future. God does not want you to be stuck in the past. He does not want you stuck in a hurtful, depressed, lonely, bitter, or stressful place. God wants to move you from that place. The first step is yours. The Bible says: **I call heaven and earth to witness against you today, that I have set before you life and death, blessing and curse. Therefore, choose life, that you and your offspring may live** (Deuteronomy 30:19).

Chapter 3

THE PROCESS

How great is God that He would give us choices? In the Kingdom of God, we are not under a dictatorship. God gave us a democracy in our faith. He gave us a right to choose. I know that can be difficult.

I remember when I was faced with a hard choice. I wanted God to treat me like I treated my children and choose for me— just like I did when they were minors. I wanted God to simply take it away. I wanted Him to give me the ability overnight to make the right choices. I expected God to change situations overnight. I needed God to heal my pain and erase the results of my bad choices immediately. I did not want to walk through the situations that my decisions caused.

The same is true for bad situations that happen that we have no control over. As a child, I could not prevent the physical and mental abuse that was inflicted. Children often become victims of people who are supposed to care for and nurture them.

Unfortunately, the abuse of children still happens every day. When a child becomes an adult, sometimes it can take years for that child to recover emotionally from the abuse. This is true for any kind of injustice experienced by an innocent person. The sad part is, people have become victims of all kinds of abuse. What's wonderful is that God is able to heal you from it all if you allow Him to come into your heart.

When people experience trauma, the first thing that shuts down is the heart. Hurt people tend to harden their hearts toward other people. They do this in order to protect themselves. Many times, hurt people will open their hearts to the wrong relationships, though not intentionally. Since hurt and pain is so familiar to them, it seems normal. In both cases, people need to become "unstuck" through the freeing power of God.

As I said earlier, God can perform heart surgery on us. That is how God healed me from the physical and mental abuse I experienced from my mother; however, walking out that pain was a totally different process. It took time for me to learn how to build a relationship with my mother despite her mental limit-ations. It was a process for me to learn how to love my mother aside from the hurt and pain of my childhood. It took some time for me to relate to her pain and to love her past what she experienced in her own childhood. The Bible reads: **Love is patient and kind; love does not envy or boast; it is not arrogant or rude. It does not insist on its own way; it is not irritable or resentful; it does not rejoice at wrongdoing, but rejoices with the truth. Love bears all things, believes all things, hopes all things, endures all things. Love never ends. As for prophe-cies, they will pass away; as for tongues, they will cease; as for know-ledge, it will pass away** (1 Corinthians 13:4-8).

I made a decision at the age of 16 to love my mother. I would not recommend jumping back into a relationship with someone who hurt you physically or mentally without first getting wisdom from God or guidance from a trusted source. When I was 16, God supernaturally shifted my heart towards my mother and gave me a heart of flesh.

I am believing that God will supernaturally heal your heart towards your parents if they have caused any pain. It is the will of God that children love their parents and for parents to love their children. The Bible says: **Honor your father and your mother, that your days may be long in the land that the Lord your God is giving you** (Exodus 20:12). I understand how this can be difficult if the abuse was a part of your childhood; however, it is still God's desire that we love and honor our parents.

God also wants parents to love their children. The Bible reads: **Fathers, do not provoke your children, lest they become discouraged** (Colossians 3:21). This scripture is telling parents to not provoke children or cause unnecessary pain.

The Bible also says: **For God so loved the world, that he gave his only Son, that whoever believes in him should not perish but have eternal life** (John 3:16). God expressed His love as a parent through His Son, Jesus Christ. Jesus expressed His love for humanity by dying on the cross for all of our sins. Jesus was innocent but He chose to die for us. The Bible reads: **For our sake he made him to be sin who knew no sin, so that in him we might become the righteousness of God** (2 Corinthians 5:21.

I understand that forgiveness can be very difficult. Sometimes, holding on to the hurt feels good. If you choose to forgive your parents, it will help your life in so many other ways.

I am a witness that forgiving my parents has enriched my life. It released me from an internal pain that only God Himself could heal. I had to forgive my parents.

Who are the people in your life that you need to forgive? I pray that you would allow the Holy Spirit to walk you through the process of forgiveness. I have heard many times that forgiveness does not mean restoration of all relationships, and this is a fact. Forgiveness frees your heart to love and allows you to become unstuck. God's desire is for you to grow in love. Unforgiveness hinders our love and faith walk.

The process of forgiveness can be frustrating. It's almost as if one day you forgive the one who hurt you, and the next day you remember what happened and hate them all over again. This is called "THE PROCESS."

We live in a fast-paced world. We can communicate instantly via phone or text messages. We also have instant messaging on social media.

We no longer have to watch our favorite TV shows on the scheduled date or at a certain time. We can record them to watch at our convenience.

The world we live in has created a microwave society. That has many benefits; however, some things still remain the same. We can't always speed up the process of healing from our past. We have to allow our minds and hearts to be renewed in time. The Bible says: **Do not be conformed to this world, but be transformed by the renewal of your mind, that by testing you may discern what is the will of God, what is good and acceptable and perfect** (Romans 12:2). This scripture clearly instructs us to allow the Holy Spirit to work out the process in our minds, hearts, and emotions.

"THE PROCESS" for everyone is different. Let me explain... The hurt and pain I experienced from the abuse I suffered from my mother was supernaturally healed by God. Even so, the hurt I experienced from my father not being around to protect me took a long time. I would take it upon myself to take care of my parents. In many ways, I became a parental figure to both of them at the age of 18.

I did not know I was holding such hurt and pain towards my father until after I had my second child out of wedlock. I had to do a lot of soul-searching and I realized that I was holding on to negative feelings and emotions towards my father. I never expressed the pain because of the love and respect I had for him. God clearly showed me how hurt I was.

The process of forgiving my father did not happen overnight. Because my father suffered from drug addiction, I had to set boundaries with him. God walked me through the process of setting limitations with my father and releasing him to God. It was not my responsibility to make sure he was in rehabilitation centers. It was not my job to make sure that he was not using drugs. I would even go to crack house, banging on doors looking for my father, all while having children of my own to take care of.

God released me from that responsibility and I became unstuck. Ironically, after I put my father in God's hands and began to pray for him, he finally got off of drugs. He got himself together and even purchased his first home! When I let go physically and continued to pray and trust God, He took care of my father while healing my personal father wounds. I was free!

God released me to love myself. I was able to focus on my children, be a good mother to them, and put them first. I was free to say "no" when boundaries were crossed. That was a life-changing lesson for me.

I took my hands off of my parents and placed them in the hands of the Lord. This allowed me time and space to grow as a woman and mother. I grew spiritually and emotionally. I allowed the Holy Spirit to teach me things. I got into the Word of God, and began a prayer life. During that time, I even started a business that got me featured in top magazine publications!

It is amazing what you can accomplish when you take the time to allow the Holy Spirit to minister to you through the Word. The Bible says: **This Book of the Law shall not depart from your mouth, but you shall meditate on it day and night, so that you may be careful to do according to all that is written in it. For**

then you will make your way prosperous, and then you will have good success (Joshua 1:8).

It is perfectly fine to love yourself. Sometimes when you have been mistreated all your life, "THE PROCESS" of loving yourself takes time. Give yourself time to learn how to love and protect yourself.

God will teach you through His Word. When I started to really understand what the Word of God said about me and who I was, I began to see myself as worthy of being loved by myself and others. The Bible reads: **But you are a chosen people, a royal priesthood, a holy nation, God's special possession, that you may declare the praises of him who called you out of darkness into his wonderful light** (1 Peter 2:9). I never saw myself as royal. Jesus is a King. Since we are born again into His kingdom, that make us royal as well!

We are a chosen people. God chose to send His Son to die for you and me. If nobody else wants you, I am here to tell you that God already chose you. We are special to God and worthy of His love.

Take a minute and read that last paragraph again. Meditate on it. It may not register the first time you read it.

The Bible says: **A new commandment I give to you, that you love one another: just as I have loved you, you also are to love one another** (John 13:34). Just as Christ wants us to love one another, you must also love yourself. When you begin to love yourself, you start making wiser choices. When you love yourself, you don't get into a relationship just to pass the time. When you love yourself, you take care of your mental state and will not engage in unnecessary conversations that don't benefit you or others. When you love yourself, you take the time to learn how to manage your emotions. When you love yourself, you do not allow other people—no matter who they are— to take advantage of you.

"THE PROCESS" of loving yourself does take time. Grant yourself the time needed to love yourself and grow.

I remember being single for four years and not dating taking time to love myself. I had to allow the Holy Spirit to help me grow. I was able to accomplish so much during that time.

It will not be easy to set boundaries and take time for yourself, but as you begin reading the Bible and developing a prayer life, you will begin to love spending quality time with God. You will begin to protect your time and be more selective about who you choose to spend it with. These are the seasons when spiritual identification takes place and God begins to tell you who you are and why you were created. This is when God begins to show you the spiritual gifts that He gave you while you were still in your mother's womb. These are the times when winners and leaders are developed.

Self-care and soul care are important in every person's life. As I get older, I am learning how to care for myself better. The Holy Spirit has given me wisdom in that area.

When we allow God to really **Father** us, He begins to teach us things we may have missed from our biological parents. God knows exactly what we need and when we need it.

I want to encourage you to trust God with you heart. Begin to spend time in prayer and time in the Word of God. It is through spending time with God that you begin to develop a real relationship with Him.

Chapter 4

THE SHIFT

When we consider things from God's perspective, the world seems like a much smaller place. I remember getting a prophetic word in 2014 that God was going to send me to the nations to preach. When I first received that word, it seemed far beyond what I could think or imagine. Since 2014 God has placed people in my life that are doing exactly that. They are preaching and teaching all over the world and inspiring people.

I have traveled internationally on four occasions since receiving that prophetic decree. In fact, I have planned my first international conference for 2020! God has completely shifted my life and ministry. In 2016, I embraced that call and God began to open doors. He placed people in my life to help me accept the assignment.

I am not sharing this with you based on something I heard. I have experienced these things firsthand. I had to trust the word of God when nothing around me lined up with what I was believing Him for. The process was necessary to get me "unstuck" in order to move into the perfect plan God has for my life.

As I reflect on my journey, I am glad that I learned how to forgive people— myself included. I've learned not to take issues and situations personally.

God will teach you not to take things to heart and how to protect it. The Bible reads: **Above all else, guard your heart, for everything you do flows from it** (Proverbs 4:23). God will teach you how to protect yourself and your emotions. He will warn you about certain people and relationships that are harmful. Even so, we have to make the choice to listen to God's instructions for our lives.

God is not going to do what He gave us the power to do for ourselves. The Bible reminds us: **Listen to my instruction and be wise; do not disregard it** (Proverbs 8:33). God wants to give us wisdom to govern our lives. We do not have

to walk around aimlessly, allowing anything and everyone access to our lives.

Remember that we are a part of a royal
priesthood. Someone can't just walk up to
Buckingham Palace in London, England
and walk right in. There are guards standing at the gates to protect the palace. If
you want to take a tour of the palace, you
have to submit your information and pay
a fee to get in.

Jesus paid the price for your salvation.
He paid the price for your heart not to be
troubled, so please don't allow anyone to
just walk in and out of your life whenever
they want to. This means we also have a
responsibility to protect our hearts and
minds.

Refuse to allow negative thoughts to
take root. Develop the habit of aborting
negativity out of your mind. Your mind is
not a dumping place. As the Bible
says: **Finally, brothers and sisters,
whatever is true, whatever is noble,
whatever is right, whatever is pure,
whatever is lovely, whatever is
admirable—if anything is excellent or**

praiseworthy—think about such things (Philippians 4:8).

The Bible is very clear about how we should think. The shift in your heart and mind will take time, so allow yourself to create habits of clearing clutter from your mind. Meditating on God's Word is the perfect place to start.

The Word of God is powerful and anointed. It is able to penetrate your heart and mind. The Bible says: **Who is this King of glory? The LORD strong and mighty, the LORD mighty in battle** (Psalm 24:8). The Word of God is inspired by God. He is able to transform you as you read His Word and focus on what He says and thinks about you.

One of my favorite scriptures when I am feeling low or a problem arises beyond my human limitations is: **But you belong to God, my dear children. You have already won a victory over those people, because the Spirit who lives in you is greater than the spirit who lives in the world** (1 John 4:4). When I read this, I feel powerful. God, the Creator of heaven and earth, decided to put His spirit of love, power, peace, and authority inside of me.

The world will try to plant all kinds of ideas and philosophies within you—all of which are meaningless and lead to a destructive end. Allow God to place love, wisdom, and knowledge in you. The process will take time; however, working out also takes time before you start seeing results. There are some things God will change instantly, but there are others that will take time.

Transformation may not be an easy process for those who don't like change. I often tell others that I am a very consistent person. This is a great quality; however, God's people cannot be committed to doing the same thing that is not producing effective results. We must pray and ask God concerning any areas in our lives that require adjustments so we can be in proper alignment with His plans.

When a car is not properly aligned it does not run very well. Misalignment can be dangerous and literally cause other problems for the vehicle. We need to ensure that our lives are in alignment.

We cannot remain stuck in old habits that are not beneficial. We can get stuck in relationships that are not fruitful. We can get stuck in careers when God clearly wants us to advance. That is why we must maintain an active prayer life to make sure that we are aligned properly in every area of our lives. When we take inventory of our lives and are properly aligned, we are ready for God to shift us from one dimension to another.

God cares about every area of our lives. When God is doing something new in my life, He always shifts things around. I had relationships that I had to release or put into proper perspective. I had to let go of old habits and mindsets. I even had to make adjustments to my schedule.

The shift that God required for me was not easy, but it was worth it. We have to let go and allow God to move things around. Believe that His plan is best and His way are above ours. The Bible reminds us: **As the heavens are higher than the earth,** so are my ways higher than your ways and my thoughts than your thoughts (Isaiah 55:9).

The truth is, shifting is always happening. The earth rotates daily. How amazing is it that we serve a God who is active and alive every day? He is working on our behalf consistently. The Bible tells us: **Indeed, he who watches over Israel will neither slumber nor sleep** (Psalm 121:4). This scripture assures us that our God is living, active, aware, and ready to assist us in any situation.

We always think about God in emergency and crisis situations, but God also wants to be involved in our desires. The Bible reads: **Take delight in the LORD, and he will give you the desires of your heart** (Psalm 37:4). My children have no problem asking me for the things they want and need. My 12-year-old lets me know when she needs pencils and pens for school; she does the same thing when she has a class trip. My daughter may ask for new shoes or sneakers even if I purchased her sneakers two months before.

The Bible says: **Truly, I say to you, unless you turn and become like children, you will never enter the kingdom of heaven** (Matthew 18:3). My daughter tells me when she is not feeling well so that I can pray for her or give her medicine. She has times when she asks me to play with her. She does not limit her requests to emergency situations.

Why is it that when we become adults, we limit our requests to our Heavenly Father? We put God in a box reserved for emergencies. We become adults and lose our "childlike faith." God wants us to come to Him like a child.

Young children believe everything their parents tells them. This is why it is important to speak the truth to your children even at a young age. God delights in our asking. I had to quit telling my daughter to stop asking me for things. I realized I was killing her ability to believe that she would get them. I told her, "It's ok to ask. You may not always receive it when you want it, but continue to ask."

This is the same position we need to take with our Lord Jesus Christ. The Bible says: **Ask, and it will be given to you; seek, and you will find; knock, and it will be opened to you** (Matthew 7:7). This is one of my favorite scriptures about asking. He wants us to ask and keep making requests. The problem is that many of us ask but if we don't get what we want right away, we lose faith and become discouraged.

I want to encourage you to get unstuck and ask the Heavenly Father for exactly what you want! God is a good parent. If we want something that we do not need immediately, He blesses us when the time is right. If it is something that we do not need at all, He will not grant it to us. It's as simple as that.

We have to trust God in our asking and in His giving. One of my husband's favorite saying is, "You can't out give God." I can tell you countless times that I prayed and asked God for things. In due season, He doubled what I prayed for.

God loves you dearly and wants you to live a blessed life, despite any challenges. The process will bring on the shift to launch you in the right direction. I believe that God is positioning you for greater, but He has to get things aligned in your life first. These are the growing pains of success that many people don't want to endure. These milestones are necessary for you to walk into your destiny.

It is also important to not miss any steps in the process. Many people grow up in the public eye, such as child actors. Later, when they become adults, the world is watching them in an attempt to become unstuck.

It is a blessing that God's love and protection shields us from public shame. It is imperative that people living their lives in the public eye have a good perception of who they are beyond the big stage. Many times, public figures allow the stage to define who they are. Trust me; I know firsthand.

I climbed the ladder of success in my last business and made it a goal to get on the award stage every year for my accomplishments. I almost let those awards define who I was as a person. I had to take a step back, rethink my values, and decide what was really important for me and my life.

There is nothing wrong with achieving goals and awards for hard work; however, we should not let accolades and public praise define who we are in Christ Jesus. We are to be thankful for our work being recognized and for God rewarding our work. We are valued because of our work, but we also bring value to our work.

Who God created us to be is why we are able to excel and succeed. All the glory goes back to Jesus Christ. The Bible reads: **You are worthy, our Lord and God, to receive glory and honor and power, for you created all things, and by your will they were created and have their being** (Revelation 4:11).

God gets the glory in everything we do. Whether we are employees, building a business, or leading a ministry, God gets the glory. When we are raising a family and our children become successful, we thank God for giving us wisdom to raise them for His glory. When we have a successful marriage and God uses it to inspire people and help other married couples, God receives the Glory. When we graduate from school with or without honors, the Glory belongs to God. All Glory and honor belong to Him.

I am not saying that you should not be honored or recognized for your work; however, the work does not define who you are. You are precious to God. Your work will pass away, but your soul will live forever. The Bible says: **I once thought these things were valuable, but now I consider them worthless because of what Christ has done** (Philippians 3:7).

Paul was an educated man from the right part of town. He was also very popular and accomplished. Paul counted all his accomplishments as nothing compared to the work and the Glory of Jesus Christ. He wrote: **Yes, everything else is worthless when compared with the infinite value of knowing Christ Jesus**

my Lord. For his sake I have discarded everything else, counting it all as garbage, so that I could gain Christ and become one with him. I no longer count on my own righteousness through obeying the law; rather, I become righteous through faith in Christ. For God's way of making us right with himself depends on faith (Philippians 3:8-9). I believe that when we take the position that Paul took regarding our work versus who the world says we are, God can give us an eternal legacy.

When we put our achievements and ambitions in the right order, God can even let our worldly legacy remain even when we are dead and gone. God can allow the work or our hands to endure and grant us the ability to maintain a good reputation for generations.

Many great people that are skillful in their vocations have very dysfunctional personal lives. Our God can help us work out the hurtful and sometimes painful details of our experiences to leave a good future for ourselves. He can give us the kind of reputations that our children and grandchildren can be proud of. The Bible states: **A good person leaves an inheritance for their children's children, but a sinner's wealth is stored up for the righteous** (Proverbs 13:22).

I believe that we are living in a time when it is amazing to be in Christ Jesus. I know that many people may not believe this, but I think differently. We have so many resources available to us that many of the old-time believers did not have. When we use the right resources the right way, God can get the victory and the glory.

When shifting occurs in our lives, it is to take us to another place. I read an article in which a woman's husband passed away. She said it was the worst time of her life; however, she was able to find peace with his passing because he was a man of God. She was not going to let a tragedy in her life prevent her from giving honor and Glory to God.

If we allow God to change the way we see things, we can grow to give God the Glory in any situation—even painful ones.

According to the Scripture: **And we know that for those who love God all things work together for good, for those who are called according to his purpose** (Romans 8:28). I focus on this verse every time I find myself in a situation that is uncomfortable or when a personal crisis hits my family. I have learned through experience to immediately go into prayer and seek the presence of God for wisdom and direction.

Chapter 5

WALKING IN IT

After a shift has taken place in our lives, we have to walk in the purpose God has for us. It may seem like we are suddenly living the life, building the business, thriving in ministry, working the career, having great relationships with our children, or even marrying the person of our dreams. However, many times when purpose happens and we finally become unstuck from the place we were, we don't have instructions. We look for help or support and find little, or none at all. This can cause feelings of fear and make us want to retreat or even return to the comfortable place we were in before. This is also a trick the devil has used for years and it has worked. It does not have to work with you.

Problems can surface when people are living their dream lives but have not taken the time to work on themselves. Many have not healed from childhood trauma or pain and end up living a nightmare. I pray that by the end of this book, you will become unstuck in all areas of your life through the power of the Holy Spirit!

God wants us to have victory in every area of our lives. I have to admit that the process takes time, and sometimes can last for extended periods. However, we make daily progress with every step we take in the right direction.

When we pray, God hears our prayers even if we don't see immediate results. When we submit to the Lord even when it does not feel good, we are making progress. Doing what's right and making wise choices is a behavior that will benefit our lives forever.

When we read the story of the children of Israel in the Bible, God shifted them out of slavery. During their "process" on the way to the promised land, they kept making the wrong choices and disobeying God. The Bible records: **So they laid it up till morning, as Moses command-ed; and it did not stink, nor were there**

any worms in it. Then Moses said, "Eat that today, for today is a Sabbath to the Lord; today you will not find it in the field. Six days you shall gather it, but on the seventh day, the Sabbath, there will be none" (Exodus 16:24-25).

These were clear instructions from Moses for the children of Israel; however, they were stuck in a slave mentality and chose not to follow the path of God to the promised land. The Bible reads: **Now it happened that some of the people went out on the seventh day to gather, but they found none. And the Lord said to Moses, "How long do you refuse to keep My commandments and My laws?"** (Exodus 16:27-28). As a result, they stayed in the process longer than they should have. A journey that should have taken only 40 days took 40 years!

Making the right choices is critical for becoming unstuck and walking through the process. I don't know about you, but I do not have 40 years to waste! When the wrong thing has happened to you, it takes everything in you to make the right choice.

61

There are stages in life. When we are born, we are newborns, then we become toddlers, children, and teenagers. Living out your dreams has stages and walking into your purpose has stages. The Bible says: **I gave you milk, not solid food, for you were not yet ready for it. Indeed, you are still not ready** (1 Corinthians 3:2). Apostle Paul called the Corinthians "infants" in the Christian life, because they were not spiritually ready or mature.

This is what happens when we skip the process. We repeat the steps until we get it right. God wants us to live a life that is flowing with blessings and to obtain new revelations and benefits at every stage.

My father would always tell me, "Baby, you only get 15 minutes of fame." I translate to say that life is short, and we have use what we have been given to make the best life we can here on earth. God is willing and able to help us develop in the areas we need to will help us "walk in it" more confidently and effectively.

The last thing we want to do is get stuck in a season. God does not want that for us.

He wants us to progress in life. The Bible reads: **Beloved, I wish above all things that thou mayest prosper and be in health, even as thy soul prospereth** (3 John 2:5).

Let me be clear. In our relationships, He wants us to prosper. In our health, He wants us to prosper. In our finances, He wants us to prosper. In learning His word and in our spiritual gifts, He wants us to prosper. In our businesses, He wants us to prosper. In our character, He wants us to prosper. I think you get what I am saying here. God wants us to prosper in **all** areas. It is our job to go through the process and allow ourselves to be developed, so that we can "walk in it."

Our God is a progressive God. The Bible says: **See, I am doing a new thing! Now it springs up; do you not perceive it? I am making a way in the wilderness and streams in the wasteland** (Isaiah 43:19). The problem is, most of us can't properly discern the seasons of life.

This is why being attached to the body (right church) is important. God created

63

people to live together to help each other. Being part of a local church for over 14 years has helped me tremendously in my walk with God. It has helped me to mature in the things of God and in His Word.

It is important to know that people are going to be people everywhere we go. If we develop a close relationship with God, he will align our lives with the right people. God will mature our minds and hearts towards all people—even the broken ones who attend church service every Sunday.

This is why it is extremely important to read the Word of God. We can read in God's Word about biblical relationships that went in the wrong directions. Paul and Barnabus were doing great works. Barnabus wanted to bring his cousin on the journey, but Paul rejected the idea. This developed contention between them because of John Mark (read Acts 13:13 for the entire story).

In this account, these men were clearly in a relationship with each other; however, they had a disagreement and decided not to continue their relationship anymore.

We have to approach every relationship with the right attitude. God is able to give us everything we are lacking to mature us for the next level. We have to decide that we are not going to be stuck. We have to work with the Holy Spirit so that He can help us properly navigate our lives from one level to another. This is why it is important not to skip the steps and the seasons of life.

As a single mother raising children, there were so many things I wanted to do, but I could not. My children were young and I was their sole provider. I had to focus on my children at that time and trust God that in due season, the time would come for me to accomplish my goals.

I got such a powerful word on this very same topic at a church service that gave me peace for the next 10 years while raising my girls. As a result, my oldest daughter is now a successful entrepreneur and blogger. That season of raising her was critical because I was training a child who was destined to have great influence in the earth.

The same is true for my younger daughter. She is 12 years younger than my oldest child. I have experience now to raise her in the way that will help bring out God's best in her life as well. I am sharing my personal parenting testimony because that particular season is important. If you are a parent and have goals you want to achieve but you have small children, raising your family is the best goal that you can ever have (in a healthy way).

We have to learn how to embrace our seasons the correct way. God is faithful and is well capable of helping us achieve our goals in the right season and at the right time. It is also important to know that our circumstances can help us as we grow and achieve God's perfect will for our lives.

When God heals us from past hurts and experiences, we can also help others who are dealing with some of the things God healed us from. Because of my experience as a single mother, I can advise other single mothers on how to properly raise children and curb their personal ambitions. Many single mothers do not have the support to achieve their goals, so they need to make sacrifices.

I can also help people who marry into a blended family. I am now a part of one, and have been married for 7 years. I can teach on healing from mother wounds because God has healed me. The hurts, pains, and successes of life are all tools for us to help other people.

If we allow God to heal us, He can use us to help others who are struggling. I decided a long time ago to allow my past pains to be a message of healing and God's grace. When we deal with the past, we can properly walk into purpose boldly and with authority.

God is faithful to us and will never leave us. The Bible states: **Be strong and courageous. Do not be afraid or terrified because of them, for the LORD your God goes with you; he will never leave you nor forsake you** (Deuteronomy 31:6). God's Word is true and is alive and well. If we apply it to our lives, it will not fail us. The Holy Spirit will comfort and guide us into all truth.

We will not face the same challenges at every new level like we did in the last season. God will mature us to face greater challenges for a greater reward. The Bible reads: **To much is given much will be required** (Luke 12:48). We have to trust that God will train us to do exactly what is required for our next season.

God will not bless us with goals and dreams and not provide exactly what we need to sustain them. The Bible says: **The blessing of the Lord maketh rich, and addeth no sorrow** (Proverbs 10:22). This is exactly what that scripture is talking about. Many of us get the blessing that we have been praying for, believing God for, fasting for, working hard for, and then we allow people to bring doubt and confusion into our lives. If the devil can't take our blessings, he will try to make us less effective with it. This is why we need the confidence of God to walk in it.

Let the words "walk in it" permeate your heart. I dare you to look in the mirror and tell your next level self, "Walk in it!" It will give you the next level of confidence that you need.

Chapter 6

LIVE IT

After we have learned to walk in God's perfect plan for our lives, we have to learn how to live it. This lesson is definitely needed.

We think when we reach our goals or achieve the life we've dreamed of, that we will suddenly feel more confident. We may assume that we are going to feel better or that dealing with challenges will become easier. Achieving goals does make us more confident; however, it is the PROCESS of achieving goals that brings us a new level of confidence—not the goal itself.

When we achieve our goals, we become better because of the obstacles we over-came. The challenges that we faced refin-ed us. We have to allow adversity to make us better and not bitter. Many people become bitter as a result of the process and do not realize that those experiences helped to shape their character. Our character has to be developed in order to achieve the plans God has for us.

When two people get married, they have to put away childish behavior. They must learn how to care for each another, putting their personal needs aside at times. The problem is that most marriages don't last because people don't know how to be selfless. Character building is important for a successful marriage.

The Bible says it this way: **When I was a child, I spoke and thought and reasoned as a child. But when I grew up, I put away childish things** (1 Corinthians 13:11). This makes it clear that certain outcomes will require maturity. We have to be willing to make difficult choices in order to live the life Christ died for us to have.

I believe that none of us are perfect; however, we should make it a priority to consistently grow and learn. We should never stop striving for perfection until we are seated in heavenly places. That is when we don't need to try anymore, because we will be made new by the sacrifice that Jesus Christ make for us on the cross.

The Bible states: **For we know that when this earthly tent we live in is taken down (that is, when we die and leave this earthly body), we will have a house in heaven, an eternal body made for us by God himself and not by human hands. [2] We grow weary in our present bodies, and we long to put on our heavenly bodies like new clothing. [3] For we will put on heavenly bodies; we will not be spirits without bodies. [4] While we live in these earthly bodies, we groan and sigh, but it's not that we want to die and get rid of these bodies that clothe us. Rather, we want to put on our new bodies so that these dying bodies will be swallowed up by life** (2 Corinthians 5: 1-4). Only then we can stop trying, because in heaven we will be made perfect. We don't need to put extra pressure on ourselves, we just need to stay close to God and He will guide us.

God is a kind, loving, and patient Father. As the Bible reminds us: **The**

Lord is merciful and gracious, slow to anger and abounding in steadfast love (Psalm 103:8). We can trust in His love and be confident in His guidance. He will help us to walk in His perfect will for our lives. We just have to be patient and trust His process.

As we get older and mature, we begin to understand the cycles of life. This will help us to assist others through these times. I recently visited the Bahamas and stayed with my friend's parents. While in their home, I realized they were in the empty nester stage. Their youngest child was in college. All of their other children were grown and had moved out.

I immediately started to think about how the empty nester stage is quickly approaching in my life. I started to consider my future even more. When I got back home, I started to plan more aggressively for that stage of my life.

Remember, we can learn from the life cycles of others. I had to become an expert by watching the people around me. My grandmother who raised me died when I was only 17 years old. When I became an adult, I took on a parental role in the lives of both of my parents. I had no choice but to learn from the successes and failures of others. I created a few of my own experiences that I now teach from.

Life is short and we have to live it. Life is good when we live an unstuck life, constantly growing in the things of the Lord. Life will have its share of tragedies, setbacks, hurts, and pains. In spite of it all, if we develop a plan for how to emerge after adversity, we can still move forward. Living an unstuck lifestyle should become a new normal for us.

I remember when I had just lost my mother. One month after her death, I started a new job. It took everything in me to concentrate and be successful on that job. I was determined to get out of the house and live because that is what she would have wanted me to do. This is also what I want for my children. I want them to learn, grow, and not remain stuck in grief after I leave this earth.

God understands that life has its unexpected problems, but guess what? Jesus has overcome them all! The Bible says: **I have said these things to you, that in me you may have peace. In the world you will have tribulation. But take heart; I have overcome the world** (John 16:33). God gave us this life to live it. Know that you have exactly what you need to accomplish His perfect will for your life.

God has the perfect plan already mapped out for us. Even before we were born, God has the blueprint for our lives. When align with His Word, there is no need to fear. We will not be stuck at any stage. God will ensure that we are progressively moving forward.

God is so amazing! He can take things that were meant for evil in our lives and turn them around for our good. The Bible tells us: **And we know that for those who love God all things work together for good, for those who are called according to his purpose** (Romans 8:28). God has that kind of power. That

76

same power is available to us when we give our lives to Jesus and build a relationship with Him. The Lord will make our paths straight. We don't need to worry about what is to come or look back at the past because our future is bright.

We serve a God who will teach us how to be sustained at each stage of our lives. Back when I was a single parent of two daughters, God taught me by the Holy Spirit and through other people. God wants us to grow.

The Bible reads: **Beloved, I pray that in all respects you may prosper and be in good health, just as your soul prospers** (3 John 1:2). God wants us to prosper in every way. There are times when God will ask us to slow down and move in a different direction.

I remember moving at full speed in my Mary Kay business. Through prayer, I felt God telling me to slow down in order to study His Word more. At the same time, I realized that God was leading me a new way. I had to make a choice: either I could choose to obey the direction God was leading me into, or I could stay stuck in a good place when God wanted to take me to a great place.

We have to trust that God is leading us to a better place than we currently are, even if it does not feel like it. In the season that God was asking me to slow down, my finances decreased; however, I grew so much in the Word of God and the understanding of the Kingdom of God. I began to understand the role He wanted me to play in advancing His Kingdom (you can't put a price on that). My needs were still met during that season.

God gave me creative ideas to walk into my next season of life. I had to make adjustments to move toward a better future. A huge part of becoming unstuck is to trust God and His instructions and plans. The Bible reads: **Trust in the LORD with all your heart and lean not on your own understanding; in all your ways submit to him, and he will make your paths straight** (Proverbs 3:5-6). God will help us accomplish our goals and have confidence, boldness, and tenacity while we live it. When we trust God, we trust our role in His plan for our lives. We can move confidently through every stage of our development with the help of the Holy Spirit.

I hate to see people stuck at a stage of life longer than God intended. This is even spoke about in the Bible with the man at the pool of Bethesda. Bethesda was a place where disabled people would go and wait for the season for the angel of the Lord to heal them. However, there was a man there for over 38 years. The Bible reads: **One of the men lying there had been sick for thirty-eight years** (John 5:5). I realize that everyone's timing is different, but I know 38 years is a long time to wait for anything. This man was stuck with the idea of getting healed.

I believe that he really wanted to be healed. He made his way to the pool, which I am sure took effort because he could not walk. We also read that Jesus asked him if he wanted to be healed.

The Bible says: **When Jesus saw him lying there and learned that he had**

been in this condition for a long time, he asked him, "Do you want to get well?" (John 5:6). We know that Jesus is all-knowing, so the question was actually a rhetorical one. Jesus reminded the man why he was there in the first place, which was to be healed. The man got so familiar with being sick that he was stuck in his condition when healing was available to him. Jesus would have never asked him the question if healing was not an option.

I am sure that other people were getting healed. Why did it take this man 38 years to get help? When we read his response to Jesus' question, we can clearly see why. The Bible reads: **"Sir," the invalid replied, "I have no one to help me into the pool when the water is stirred. While I am trying to get in, someone else goes down ahead of me"** (John 5:7). This is clear that he was waiting on someone to come and help him to get into the pool. I am sure someone tried to help him. That is my first thought. My second thought is that maybe God gave him instructions before to get up and, at the point of his obedience, God would have healed him. However, he was waiting for help.

The Bible says: **Then Jesus said to him, "Get up! Pick up your mat and walk"** (John 5:8). Jesus had to tell him face to face, "I am doing something different with you. You do not have to get in the pool. I am healing you right here and right now by your obedience to My instructions."

How many times do we put God in a box and look at the way He has always done things, expecting Him to show up in our lives the same way? We have to be open to unusual moves of God. We expect God to always send us someone to help us or mentor us for the next level. What if God wants to mentor you Himself? He wants to be your instructor for this particular season. He does not want anyone else to help you, He wants you to depend solely on Him.

I am not at all saying that mentors are unnecessary. I believe that all new believers and people need guidance at some point; however, I believe at some points in our lives, God will step in and give clear instructions from the throne room of Heaven.

Wisdom is available to everyone. The Bible reads: **If any of you lacks wisdom, you should ask God, who gives generously to all without finding fault, and it will be given to you** (James 1:5). This scripture is one of my favorites because life can present situations for which we need the wisdom of God to help us. Sometimes we won't have the answer. We need His wisdom.

The wisdom of God is available to all of us. All we need to do is ask God and He will give it to us generously. We have to humble ourselves in prayer and the Maker of the world will give us wisdom. This alone is a reason to praise God and be confident in Him as He leads and directs our lives.

I am so excited to be a part of His kingdom and to be called a child of God! The Bible say: **But to all who did receive him, who believed in his name, he gave**

the right to become children of God (John 1:12). This privilege of being a part of the family of God gives us access to the kingdom and His power. These kingdom privileges are available to us, because of the great work that Jesus did and the sacrifice He made on the cross when He died for us:

The Bible reads: **For Christ also suffered once for sins, the righteous for the unrighteous, that he might bring us to God, being put to death in the flesh but made alive in the spirit** (1 Peter 3:18). We also can celebrate the fruit of the Spirit and the suffering that our Lord and Savior endured for us. The Bible says: **But the fruit of the Spirit is love, joy, peace, patience, kindness, goodness, faithfulness, gentleness, self-control; against such things there is no law** (Galatians 5:22-23). We can grow in these things we can live it for the world to see. We can be the perfect example of what Jesus Christ did on the cross.

We are not perfect, but we are all a work in progress. We can exhibit the fruit of the

Spirit even when it is difficult or unpopular to do so. God will help us as we grow from glory to glory. The Bible tells us: **And we all, with unveiled face, beholding the glory of the Lord, are being transformed into the same image from one degree of glory to another. For this comes from the Lord who is the Spirit** (2 Corinthians 3:18).

God wants us to go from one degree of glory to another depending on the assignment that He has for us. He does not want us stuck; however, He understands that people can get stuck. I wrote this book because I have been stuck a few times in my life. I wanted to offer tools through the Holy Spirit and by sharing my testimony of how I was rescued from a stuck place and released into a new place of freedom.

God uses ordinary people to spread His promise of freedom and redemption. The Bible reminds us: **But God chose what is foolish in the world to shame the wise; God chose what is weak in the world to shame the strong** (1

Corinthians 1:27). You do not need to be perfect for God to use you; simply be obedient.

When we obey God, there is nothing we cannot do through Christ. God can fully depend on us to accomplish His agenda when He knows that He can trust us.

When we read about the life of Job, God suggested to the devil that he tempt his servant. The Bible says: **And the Lord said to Satan, "Have you considered my servant Job, that there is none like him on the earth, a blameless and upright man, who fears God and turns away from evil? He still holds fast his integrity, although you incited me against him to destroy him without reason"** (Job 2:3). God was confident in his servant Job, knowing that he would not break under pressure to the point that He suggested to the devil to consider him.

Can God depend on our faithfulness to be tested in hard seasons to get us to the other side of glory? We can study the characteristics of Job so that when times of testing come, we can take on the posture of Job and receive the reward after our trial. I am so happy that God delights in helping His children and restoring us. When we read the entire account of Job's experience, God restored Job with even more than he lost. This is the nature of our God.

Chapter 7

GROW IT

When times of testing come in our lives and we get on the other side, we can rejoice! I have found that during seasons of immediate breakthrough, God gives us peace. We are no longer stressed, worried, or anxious.

We know from the Bible and the previous chapter that peace is a fruit of the Spirit. The Bible says: **But the fruit of the Spirit is love, joy, peace, patience, kindness, goodness, faithfulness, gentleness, self-control; against such things there is no law** (Galatians 5:22-23). It is safe to say that after a trial God gives us peace. After God restored Job, He blessed him with twice as much as he had before. The Bible reads: **The Lord restored the fortunes of Job when he prayed for his friends, and the Lord gave Job twice as much as he had before** (Job 42:10). We can see from the text that often after a trial, God sends restoration.

This is the hard part for most people. After the trial is over, they get stuck in the devastation of the experience and never cross over to victory. When we receive a breakthrough, we should immediately start petitioning God for restoration. The Bible says: **I will repay you for the years the locusts have eaten—the great locust and the young locust, the other locusts and the locust swarm—my great army that I sent among you** (Joel 2:25). God is so powerful that only He can restore time.

Almost everything can be restored— relationships, homes, cars—but only God can restore time. God can restore the time and place you in an even better position than you were before! We serve a loving God who understands us and the challenges we face. The Bible reads: **For we do not have a high priest who is unable to empathize with our weaknesses, but we have one who has been tempted in**

every way, just as we are—yet he did not sin (Hebrews 4:15).

Our Lord and Savior, Jesus Christ, understand the sins and the temptations we endure in everyday life. This is why Jesus came to earth in a human body to experience what we face. We serve a Savior who identifies with our struggles. We often serve people who have no real awareness of our true circumstances; however, Jesus understands them all.

When I was a single mother, I had to depend on Jesus to give me wisdom concerning how to provide for my children. I would pray and God would always send provision for us. I can honestly say that God is a Provider. I have seen the hand of God move in my life in the area of finances when I needed provision. I had no other choice but to depend on Him.

The Bible says: **But seek first his kingdom and his righteousness, and all these things will be given to you as well** (Matthew 6:33). The Word is clear that if we put the kingdom of God first, when we pray, we can ask for anything and

God will give it to us. The truth is, when we are living a lifestyle that pleases God, our prayers will line up with His plan for our lives. When we are in alignment with the Word of God, our hearts will be in accordance with God's.

We don't need to worry about asking for wrong things when our lives are properly aligned. God will place burden on our heart so that when we pray, we will ask according to what He desires. This is a win-win situation! The Bible reads: **The steps of a good man are ordered by the Lord: and he delighteth in his way** (Psalm 37:23). This is confirmation that when we walk with God, He will order our steps. This may be hard to understand or comprehend if you do not have a history with God; however, if you start today, He will help you establish your faith and belief system.

When I find myself in difficult situations and my faith is being tested, I often remember how God showed up on my behalf before. This is what having a history with God will do for you. Once you've experienced answered prayers, it will give you more faith for your next assignment, trial, or situation.

It's exciting to receive answers from God! You will begin to find other people with which to share testimonies about your answered prayers. You will even find other people who are believing God for answers and you will join your faith with theirs.

The power of prayer is contagious! The Bible says: **And God blessed them. And God said to them, "Be fruitful and multiply and fill the earth and subdue it and have dominion over the fish of the sea and over the birds of the heavens and over every living thing that moves on the earth"** (Genesis 1:28). It is God's desire that we multiply in everything we do, including our faith.

It is important to know that God will help us grow in faith; however, we do have a few responsibilities. To grow it, we must pray and read the Word of God. When we read the Word of God, it will give us encouragement as we read about how God helped the saints in biblical times.

God will make Himself available in our present situation and help us in every area of life, all with have to do is ask. The Bible reads: **If any of you lacks wisdom, let him ask God, who gives generously to all without reproach, and it will be given him** (James 1:5). There's no need to stress out over situations or things we don't know the answers to. We must pray and God will give us wisdom.

I needed the wisdom of God in a situation I faced. I had not heard from my father in a few weeks and I was concerned. My father has a history of drug abuse so, when I did not hear from him in the past, I would immediately go to his home to make sure that he was fine. A no-call from my father in the past meant that he was in trouble. I decided to take a trip to North Carolina just to make sure everything was ok with my father; however, when I prayed about it, I could sense that God did not want me to go.

Reluctantly, I listened to the unction of the Holy Spirit. My husband had taken some vacation time, so we rented a car because we did not want to put extra mileage on our own. When we prayed, God changed our plans.

I wanted to go, but I had peace knowing that my father was fine. How did this peace come? When we listened to God and stayed home, I felt peace enter my heart. I felt like God was saying, *"Cynthia it's a new season. You don't have to run after or look for your father. Rest in Me and I will take care of him."* I also felt like the parental role I had assumed in my father's life was over. God was retiring me from being responsible for my father. That was the wisdom of God.

After prayer, the peace felt good. God's wisdom had given me freedom! A few weeks later, my father called me. He said that he was doing fine and just needed some mental space from the outside world. I was happy to hear from him, but I had peace already from my Heavenly Father.

That experience gave me even greater faith. I can now use that situation as a source of comfort when I feel worried or concerned. This is how we grow our faith.

When God blesses us with something, He also wants us to grow it. It does not matter if it's a marriage, family, business, or a new revelation in Scripture, He wants us to grow it.

There is a parable in the Bible about a wealthy man who gave talents to his workers. The Bible reads: **For it will be like a man going on a journey, who called his servants and entrusted to them his property. To one he gave five talents, to another two, to another one, to each according to his ability. Then he went away. He who had received the five talents went at once and traded with them, and he made five talents more. So also he who had the two talents made two talents more. But he who had received the one talent went and dug in the ground and hid his master's money** (Matthew 25:14-18). The last servant did not grow his talent, he hid it. The master was very upset with him. He was stuck in his own fears and limited his ability. Take the time to read the entire text.

That is how some of us become with the gifts, talents, and abilities God gives us. We sit on them and don't use them. Many people can sing, but don't use their voices. Many can write, but don't use their gifts. Many can prophesy, but won't open their mouths in obedience. Others can draw, but don't put their gifts to use.

When God blesses us with a gift, we have to grow it. We can't neglect the talent and anointing God places within us. The Bible says: **The Spirit of the Lord is upon me, because he has anointed me to proclaim good news to the poor. He has sent me to proclaim liberty to the captives and recovering of sight to the blind, to set at liberty those who are oppressed, to proclaim the year of the Lord's favor** (Luke 4:18:19). The anointing is to activate and move us forward. God's desire is for us to use the anointing and gifts to advance the kingdom of God.

God blesses us with gifts and talents to use them to advance His Kingdom and to grow it.

By reading this book, you are doing the work that it takes to grow. Please do not get stuck in the idea of being unstuck. When you finish this book, God is going to bring to your memory a few places in your own life that you have become stagnant. Once you receive freedom from the Holy Spirit, get to work. Thank God for releasing you into a new season and for freeing up your heart.

Everyone will not move at the same pace. One of the jobs of the enemy of our souls is get us caught up in comparison. The enemy will despise the new liberty you received and will do everything in his power to stop it. He often does this through comparison.

Do not compare your progress with anyone else's, and don't allow other people to do it to you. People will often compare you to others because they don't have an identity themselves. Please do not hold it against them. Many are searching for their identity in Christ Jesus, but have not yet been healed or set free from worldly standards. That alone is a process.

You don't have to have it all figured out. God will send encouragers and mentors to help you along the way. You are special to God, which is why no two people have the same fingerprint. The Bible says: **For we are God's masterpiece. He has created us anew in Christ Jesus, so we can do the good things he planned for us long ago** (Ephesians 2:10). When we are in Christ, He has things that he wants us to do.

The work He had designed for each person may be different. One person may start a journal and write down the new things God is teaching, while another person may join a ministry at church. Everyone's work is different.

It is important to ask God what your next move should be in this season. Refuse to remain in the same place you were when you started this book. God has plans for your life. The Bible reads: **"For I know the plans I have for you," declares the**

LORD, "plans to prosper you and not to harm you, plans to give you hope and a future" (Jeremiah 29:11).

It may be hard for you to truly embrace that God has a plan for your life, but He does. I remember being a single mother of two small kids. God's plan for me at that time was to raise my children to love both God and others so they could be the type of godly women He desired. That alone is a job, and an honorable one!

Please don't think that your assignment is undesirable or does not matter. It does. God is taking note of everything that you are doing and He loves you. Please be patient with yourself because your Heavenly Father is patient with you.

God celebrates every move you make to improve and grow in the knowledge of who He has created you to be. I pray the wisdom of God will give you the foundation and structure you need to grow in every area. The Bible says: **Being confident of this, that he who began a good work in you will carry it on to completion until the day of Christ Jesus**

(Philippians 1:6). You are God's master-piece and He will finish what He started in you.

It is reassuring to know that God is patient with us and He teaches us how to be patient with one another. The Bible reads: **Love is patient, love is kind. It does not envy, it does not boast, it is not proud** (1 Corinthians 13:4). Don't listen to the voices in your head that speak against what God said about you. The negative voices are not from God; they are rooted in evil and destruction.

I know about those negative voices. My negative voices came from my childhood. When I became an adult, they came from the choices I made. When I continued to make wrong choices, those voices grew louder. When I submitted myself to the Lord, they slowly begin to disappear. Negative voices may continue to pop up every now and then, but we have a weapon against them through prayer and the Word of God.

Other things that would try to stop you on your journey toward becoming unstuck are feelings of fear and worthlessness. Someone told me years ago, if the devil can't steal your blessing, he will try to make you unhappy with it. That really helped me because I would often get blessed in a certain area of my life but then experience opposition and warfare in that area.

As a young Christian, I did not know about spiritual warfare. Opposition would often try to make me give up on anything positive I was working toward. Once I started to grow in my walk with God and read the Scriptures, God sent seasoned Christians to share their experiences concerning spiritual warfare.

After reading the Bible about all the trials the people endured and then hearing from my Christian brothers and sisters, I was confident that I could conquer any opposition or warfare in prayer. This is the reason why I am writing to you about it. You have what it takes to be consistent in prayer and the power to push through it to get to a place called victory.

In my early days as a believer, this was frustrating because I was still stuck with hurt and fear in my heart. Things from my childhood still had a tight grip on my emotions. The pain of people hurting me for no reason was still affecting me. This caused me to be stuck in the area of progress. Every time I started something; I could not finish it. When opposition and spiritual warfare would arise, hurt and pain would speak to my mind instead of the Word of God. The Bible says: **Instead, let the Spirit renew your thoughts and attitudes** (Ephesians 4:23).

Praying and reading the Word of God gives us a new mind and a new spirit to fight for the things that rightfully belong to us. When we pray and study the Word of God, it chases the voices in our mind away. Negative voices, hurt, and pain can't remain in the same place the Word of God is and where healing is taking place. Those voice may seem to be stubborn when you first start to develop a prayer life, but they will soon disappear in time.

Chapter 8

REST IN IT

We can rest in God's love and be confident in His grace. No matter what comes our way, we serve a God who is actively waiting to assist us and helps us fight our battles. The Bible reads: **One of you routs a thousand, because the LORD your God fights for you, just as he promised** (Joshua 23:10).

Think about it. The Creator of the universe fights for us! This can be hard to comprehend with our natural minds; however, when we read the scriptures and then take into account of our own lives, we can be sure that God loves us.

When I think about situations in my life that could have killed me, I know that I am still alive today by the grace of God. I am sure you can recall a time when God spared your life. It is those memories that help to strengthen our faith and help us to remain grounded in Him. Resting in God shows our confidence and faith in His works.

God loves when we exhibit confidence in Him despite the situation. The Bible says: **And without faith it is impossible to please God, because anyone who comes to him must believe that he exists and that he rewards those who earnestly seek him** (Hebrews 11:6). God is so wonderful that He is patient with us and will help us grow our faith for as long as we live.

God is a loyal Father. The Bible tells us: **The LORD himself goes before you and will be with you; he will never leave you nor forsake you. Do not be afraid; do not be discouraged** (Deuteronomy 31:8). It took me time to understand this about God since I came from a dysfunctional family. I finally realized that God is not like my earthly father and will always be by my side.

When I first began having prayer time and reading my Bible, I would pray and only tell God certain things. During the course of that day or week, God would answer my prayers! God proved Himself to me when He clearly did not have to. The Bible says: **One who has unreliable friends soon comes to ruin, but there is a friend who sticks closer than a brother** (Proverbs 18:24).

Loyal committed, unshakable, and un-movable—that is who our God is! God will also grow us in these areas to be com-mitted to His Word and His Kingdom during times of trouble. We can have the same characteristics as our Creator. We can rest in the Word of God and the fullness of His glory.

God has given us everything we need to be successful. We have everything we need to be a successful parent, spouse, employee, entrepreneur, or single person. In every stage of our lives, God equips us with the tools that are already on the inside of us to become victorious; however, we may need help manifesting what He has already placed within us.

We all need a safe place to grow. My prayer is that you would find a safe place in your life and a community to grow in your spiritual journey. In the beginning, life in Christ can be challenging, but everything new has its own set of obstacles.

I love being a mother; however, at times I was challenged. When my oldest daughter became a teenager, I had to adjust my parenting style. I had to see her as a growing woman instead of a little girl. God gave me the right tools to parent my children at every stage of their lives.

I remember feeling the same way as a new wife. I waited for 35 years to finally get married, but then I had to learn how to share my life and space with another person. This was a challenge for me in the beginning, but through prayer and the wisdom of God he gave me the tools I needed to succeed.

We do not have all the answers and we don't need to know them all. We serve an all-knowing God. The Bible reads: **Great is our Lord and abundant in strength; His understanding is infinite** (Psalm 147:5). We have a Creator who has all the answers. The Bible says: **But the very hairs of your head are all numbered**

(Matthew 10:30). God knows everything about us. We can rest in His love and be assured that God knows the beginning and the end of every situation.

We can cast our cares on the One who went to the cross. The Bible reads: **Give all your worries and cares to God, for he cares about you** (1 Peter 5:7). God was aware that we would have challenges in this life, but He gave us the answers to deal with them.

We live in a world where everyone wants everything *now*. We want all the answers today and not tomorrow. We can trust the fact that even if God does not give us answers immediately, He can turn challenging and hurtful situations around for our good. The Bible says: **You intended to harm me, but God intended it for good to accomplish what is now being done, the saving of many lives** (Genesis 50:20). We must trust God, His plans, and His process.

I had to take care of myself at a very early age. My grandmother who raised me passed away when I was only 16 years old.

I was left with no other choice but to survive. Many of my friends were in similar situations.

When you are forced to fend for yourself and depend on your own decisions, it can be hard to trust God. When I was a child, I looked forward to becoming an adult so that I would be able to make my own choices. However, this was not as easy as I thought it would be. Because I did not have an example from my biological parents, I had to learn how to trust God. It did not happen overnight; it was a process that took time.

God is kind. He was and still is patient with us as we grow in trusting Him. The Bible reads: **I have told you these things, so that in me you may have peace. In this world you will have trouble. But take heart! I have overcome the world** (John 16:33). Jesus was basically telling us, *"Relax and chill out! I've got you covered."* John 16:33 can be confusing when all you know how to do is trust your own instincts. It forces us to let go of our old way of thinking and to allow God through the Holy Spirit to transform our minds.

I had to completely trust God at a particular place on my journey in the area of finances. As a single parent, I was confident that God would give me the tools I needed to make a living for my family.

My grandmother would always repeat this scripture: **I was young and now I am old, yet I have never seen the righteous forsaken or their children begging bread** (Psalm 37:25). My grandmother taught me this and she also lived by it.

When I was younger, it seemed as if my grandmother and I went shopping every weekend. She was retired (as far as I can remember), but she always had money to shop and go on vacations. I was right there with her on many of those vacations. I remember when she was preparing to go on a trip to Israel with her church. It was a big deal. Israel was mentioned in the Bible many times and I was excited for her. My grandmother's faith in God to provide for her and living the Bible in her everyday life was enough proof for me that it worked.

When she passed away, that same principle became real in my life. I lived by that scripture. Now I can see the hand of God on my finances.

My grandmother was the example. Her faith and lifestyle aligned with her faith. I used that same faith to purchase my first home as a single mother and I continue to use that faith today. However, in the last few years, God is growing me even more in the area of my finances to advance His Kingdom. It is uncomfortable, but if I am going to do everything in my heart that I desire to do for God, I am going to require new levels of faith in my finances. I cannot borrow my grandmother's faith for this task. This is going to be groundbreaking and carry a new level of generational blessings in my bloodline to create wealth through faith.

This is exactly how faith works. We can lay foundations in our families, but our children and grandchildren can take that faith to another level. That is what God wants to do for your family.

God wants to take your faith to another level so that you can leave a legacy of faith for your children and grandchildren to build on. God wants to create a spiritual inheritance that will manifest in the natural to help your family, friends, and the people around you.

In the early stages of my prayer journey, I would remind God about what He did for my grandmother. In fact, my grandmother told me that I would travel to many more places in my lifetime. I believe she was speaking her words of faith into my little 10-year-old heart. I can see her words clearly coming to pass in my life. I now speak words of life to my daughters.

God wants you to rest in His love and depend on Him for guidance. God wants you to have a generational legacy of faith in your family in every area. Will you take the time and be patient with God's supernatural plan? The Lord is waiting to partner with you on your journey.

God does not want you to remain stuck. He does not want you to be stagnant when He has advancement in mind for you and your family. The decision you make to move in another direction will also affect the lives of your children. Your family and friends will see the change. Even if they do not trust your process, they will not be able to deny your progress.

You may have to take this journey alone. That is perfectly fine. The driver is usually the first one on the bus anyway. Allow the Holy Spirit to be your GPS. He will guide you into all truth. The Bible reads: **But when he, the Spirit of truth, comes, he will guide you into all the truth. He will not speak on his own; he will speak only what he hears, and he will tell you what is yet to come** (John 16:13). There is a lot of talk about speaking your truth, but as children of the Most High God, we can speak the universal truth of God's Word that will not come back to us void. The Bible says: **So is my word that goes out from my mouth: It will not return to me empty, but will**

accomplish what I desire and achieve the purpose for which I sent it (Isaiah 55:11). God confirms His own word.

What a good, good Father! We can rest in His promises and be assured that He created us for His enjoyment. We are His masterpieces.

I have found when I read the Word of God over and over again, it gives me supernatural peace when my mind is troubled. His Word gives me strength in weary times. The Bible reads: **Come to me, all you who are weary and burdened, and I will give you rest** (Matthew 11:28).

It seemed like my grandmother was working all the time. When I woke up in the morning, she was awake before me. When I went to sleep at night, she went to bed after me. We could not sleep late in the Jeter house. There was no such thing as sleeping past 9:00 a.m., even on a Saturday—unless we were sick or worked nights. This gave me a very good work ethic. The problem was, I did not know how to relax and rest.

My husband recently gave me a revelation that rest is from God. God designed rest to give us a chance to recharge. I have to admit I struggle in this area but I have gotten much better over time. God gave me a companion that reminds me to rest.

I like to work. I believe that most people like to work or would like to find a job that they like; however, we are not validated by our work. The Bible says: **But remember the LORD your God, for it is he who gives you the ability to produce wealth, and so confirms his covenant, which he swore to your ancestors, as it is today** (Deuteronomy 8:18).

The ability to work comes from God, the success in our work comes from God, and the desire to work comes from God. When we align our lives with the will of God, He will lead us to the work that is designed for our lives. God has a specific assignment for each and every one of us at different seasons of our lives.

There was a time during my vocation when God totally changed the type of work that I was doing. I remember working in corporate America. I was thinking about going back to school or starting my own business. I prayed and God clearly told me to start the business. Seven years into entrepreneurship, God shifted me again into ministry. The work comes from God. Rest in it.

When you live a life of prayer and meditate on His Word, God will give you the strength to work. Allow God to shift you as needed. The Bible reads: **These were his instructions to them: "The harvest is great, but the workers are few. So pray to the Lord who is in charge of the harvest; ask him to send more workers into his fields"** (Luke 10:2). This includes ministry work and your occupation.

There is freedom in God's love and in His Word. The Bible says: **It is for freedom that Christ has set us free. Stand firm, then, and do not let yourselves be burdened again by a yoke of slavery** (Galatians 5:1). If you feel stuck in any way, I hope that by the time you finish this book you will have a spring-board into freedom.

My prayer is that you would deepen your prayer life and become stronger than ever before. God is shifting the earth and He is moving the people in the earth. He is raising up people who will cry out to Him concerning the next move for their lives.

If you are reading this book, it is because God has not forgotten about you. This is the season that the shift is going to take place. I believe that God has revealed some things in your heart and mind about the areas that He wants to unlock. God is releasing dreams that you gave up on years ago due to hurt and fear. This is your season for freedom and redemption.

When you are unstuck, you can feel it in your heart. Your energy level increases and you begin to have more strength. God has shaken the weight off you in the spiritual realm and now you must take the weight off in the natural. Why? Because you were bound and now you are free. You are unstuck!

You are open to God shifting you logistically in your ministry or vocation. You are standing firmly on the foundation that Jesus Christ built and you are confident that anything you do is solid on it. You are resting in the peace and glory of God.

Enjoy the freedom that you have received and get excited about it! Your life is about to change. You are stepping into God's perfect will and plan concerning your future.

Be comfortable with the process and know that you are not alone. God will complete the work He started. Rest in this hope, my friends. Rest on the promises of God. The Bible says: **For I know the plans I have for you, declares the Lord, plans for welfare and not for evil, to give you a future and a hope** (Jeremiah 29:11).

Rest in it and be happy that God is with you. He is going to do amazing things with you and through you. He is going to restore everything that was delayed or taken. It is true that God is going to give you double for your trouble! Get happy and shout, **"I am FREE and UNSTUCK!"**

CYNTHIA JETER-CLEMENTS

Cynthia Jeter-Clements is an author, entrepreneur, and minister of the Gospel. Cynthia has spoken at multiple churches, schools, corporate offices and not-for-profit organizations sharing her story of salvation and how she overcame growing up as an abused child, living with her mother that had mental issues, and supporting her drug addicted father. She also shares stories about her abusive and hurtful dating relationships before she fully submitted her life to Christ.

In 2016 she received clear direction concerning preaching and teaching. She then decided that it was time to move on the word of God and the vision He placed in her heart.

Cynthia is passionate about helping people reach their destiny and their God-given calling. She has also been featured in several magazines including **O - The Oprah Magazine, Essence, Marie Claire** and **Good Housekeeping Magazine**.

For Booking or Additional Information:

CynthiaJeterClements.org

Made in the USA
Middletown, DE
29 October 2020

22913113R00076